The Unkno

JAMES WILKINSON

The Tomb of the Unknown
Warrior, surrounded by silk
Flanders poppies, is the most
prominent in the Abbey.

The Tomb

JUST INSIDE THE ENTRANCE TO WESTMINSTER ABBEY, set into the floor, is a black marble tombstone surrounded by red poppies. Beneath it lies a soldier, unidentified by name or rank, who was killed in the First World War. He is 'The Unknown Warrior', who was buried here in 1920 as a representative of the 1·6 million men who died in battle. Was he mown down by machine-gun fire as he charged the German front line? Or did he simply drown in a shell-hole full of liquid mud? No-one will ever know.

The carnage of the First World War is evidenced by the endless rows of headstones in military cemeteries throughout western Europe. After the War many of those who mourned their husbands, brothers, sons or lovers did not even know where or how they had died and had no grave to visit. For them, the Unknown Warrior's Tomb became the focus for their grief: it was just possible that the anonymous soldier, buried in the Abbey among kings and princes, was their own kith and kin.

Today, the Tomb has become a symbol of war dead from all conflicts. Together with the annual Field of Remembrance on the green just outside the Abbey, it has become a place of pilgrimage for the bereaved.

Each year on Remembrance Sunday, representatives of the armed services, together with the Abbey clergy, choir and distinguished visitors, gather round the Tomb for the two minutes' silence, its start and finish marked by artillery fire from nearby Horse Guards Parade. In Whitehall, the two minutes' silence is observed by Her Majesty The Queen and other members of the Royal Family gathered round the Cenotaph – literally an empty tomb – which was unveiled by King George V on 11 November 1920 just before he attended the funeral of the Unknown Warrior.

Each year, in the Field of Remembrance, the public can plant a small cross in memory of a loved one who died in battle, or simply as their own personal tribute to soldiers who have sacrificed their lives. Thus, each year, the nation remembers and pays homage.

Many nations now have their own Unknown Warrior's Tomb to act as a focal point for remembrance. But how did it all begin? And whose idea was it?

The Idea

THE SUGGESTION THAT AN UNKNOWN SOLDIER from the battlefield should be brought back to Britain for burial, as a representative of all those who died, is usually credited to an army padre, the Rev'd David Railton who, in 1916, was serving on the Western front. After the War he wrote about how the idea was born:

'I came back from the line at dusk. We had just laid to rest the mortal remains of a comrade. I went to a billet in front of Erkingham, near Armentières. At the back of the billet was a small garden, and in the garden, only six paces from the house, there was a grave. At the head of the grave there stood a rough cross of white wood. On the cross was written, in deep black-pencilled letters, 'An Unknown British Soldier' and in brackets underneath 'of the Black Watch'. It was dusk and no-one was near, except some officers of the billet playing cards. I remember how still it was. Even the guns seemed to be resting. How that grave caused me to think.

'So I thought and thought and wrestled in thought. What can I do to ease the pain of father, mother, brother, sister, sweetheart, wife and friend? Quietly and gradually there came out of this mist of thought this answer clear and strong, "Let this body – this symbol of him – be carried reverently over the sea to his native land". And I was happy for about five or ten minutes.'

Railton wrote to the General Officer Commanding the British Army in France and Belgium, Sir Douglas Haig, suggesting that a body should be brought to England for burial, but he received no reply. Whether this planted the seed of the idea in official minds is not clear. We do know that Railton did nothing more until after the War was over.

When he returned from the War he was appointed Vicar of St John the Baptist Church in Margate, Kent. The idea for an unknown soldier burial nagged at him until eventually in August 1920 he wrote to the Dean of Westminster, Dr Herbert Ryle. Railton had decided that only Westminster

Abbey would be suitable for the burial as it was 'the Parish Church of the Empire'. He had originally thought of writing to King George V but apparently feared that the King's advisers would suggest the tomb should be placed in some open space like Trafalgar Square or Hyde Park. By then the idea was already germinating elsewhere. France had proposed burying a representative of its war dead in the Pantheon in Paris and a news story had been published in the Daily Express nearly a year before, on 16 September 1919, asking whether a British hero should be similarly honoured. The place suggested was beneath the Cenotaph in Whitehall –

at that time a much smaller, temporary structure. Both the Lord Mayor of London and a member of the Peace Celebrations Committee were reported to be enthusiastic about the idea.

Whether the idea would have matured without Railton's letter is a matter of conjecture. It is clear, however, that from the start Dean Ryle favoured the idea and he was in a position to push it through. He replied to Railton saying that he was not able to give an answer straight away but that the idea would 'germinate'. It 'germinated' for several weeks because it was not until 4 October that Ryle wrote to Lord Stamfordham, the King's Private Secretary, to offer an Abbey burial to an unknown soldier. He wrote, 'There are thousands of graves, I am told, of English "Tommies" who fell at the front – names not known. My idea is that one such body (name not known) should be exhumed and interred in Westminster Abbey, in the Nave.' Three days later the Dean received a not altogether enthusiastic reply from Stamfordham in which he expressed the King's reservations. 'His Majesty is inclined to think that nearly two years after the last shot was fired on the battlefields of France and Flanders is so long ago that a funeral now might be regarded as belated.' However the Dean had already enrolled the Prime Minister and General Sir Henry Wilson to his side and when the King later consulted the Prime Minister, he was persuaded that the idea would work.

On 18 October the Dean received a further letter from Stamfordham informing him of the King's approval and suggesting that the burial should take place on Armistice Day, 11 November, just over three weeks hence, giving little time to make the arrangements.

The Cabinet set up a Memorial Service Committee under Lord Curzon, the Foreign Secretary. Once the idea had been announced, the newspapers and the public gave it their full backing.

The Selection

IN 1920 THE BATTLEFIELDS IN FRANCE AND FLANDERS were still littered with the graves of those buried where they had fallen. Thousands more had no grave – their bodies long since lost in the mud. War cemeteries were being established and the long slow task of collecting the war dead from their makeshift graves for proper burial alongside their comrades was proceeding steadily.

The arrangements for the selection of the Unknown Warrior were carried out under the command of Brigadier General L J Wyatt, the General Officer Commanding troops in France and Flanders in 1920 and the Director of the War Graves Commission. Because conflicting accounts of how it was done had been circulating, in November 1939 he revealed what happened in a letter in the Daily Telegraph. He wrote that on 7 November 1920, he had given instructions that four bodies should be exhumed from each of four battle areas: the Aisne, the Somme, Arras and Ypres. Those bringing in the bodies had to choose one from a grave marked 'Unknown British Soldier' and they had to make sure that the soldier had died during the early years of the war to ensure that it could not be recognised and he had to have been wearing a British uniform. Each body was exhumed and taken to the chapel at St Pol in northern France. Brigadier General Wyatt wrote in his letter: 'Reporting to my headquarters office at St Pol, at midnight on 7 November, Col. Gell, one of my staff, announced that the bodies were in the chapel and the men who had brought them had gone. With Col. Gell I therefore entered the Chapel. The four bodies lay on stretchers, each covered with a Union Jack; in front of the altar was the shell of a coffin which had been sent from England to receive the remains. I selected one and, with the assistance of Col. Gell placed it in the shell and screwed down the lid. The other bodies were removed and reburied in the military cemetery outside my head-quarters at St Pol'.

'I had no idea even of the area from which the body I selected had come; and no one else can know it.' Thus, an ordinary soldier was chosen for burial among the greatest in the land.

The Journey

WITH THE UNKNOWN WARRIOR SELECTED, it was now time for the long journey home. This was to be a journey of extraordinary poignancy. The soldier may have been an ordinary Tommy but he was to be given a Field Marshal's burial.

Before the Warrior left the St Pol chapel there was a short service attended by chaplains from the Church of England, the Roman Catholic Church and the Non-Conformist Churches. Following this the coffin was placed in an ambulance and driven under escort to Boulogne. With it went six barrels (100 sandbags) of soil from the Ypres Salient so that, in Brigadier General Wyatt's words, 'the body should rest in the soil on which so many of our troops gave up their lives.' Outside the town the route was lined with French and British troops. As the field ambulance entered the courtyard of the old chateau of the Port of Boulogne, a group of VIPs was waiting to receive it. The bearer party of British and Dominion soldiers carried the coffin into the chateau's Chapel Ardente, where it rested overnight under guard.

Meanwhile in England a special coffin had been ordered into which the shell would be placed, and this had been sent to Boulogne to receive the remains. The coffin was made of oak from a tree which had grown in the garden of Hampton Court Palace. Around the coffin were wrought-iron bands and secured along the top of the lid was a Crusader's sword taken from the Tower of London collection. Before leaving England the coffin had been taken to Westminster Abbey where it had been placed on a pall and photographed, resting above the place where it would eventually be buried. Carved on the lid was the inscription

A BRITISH WARRIOR WHO FELL IN THE GREAT WAR 1914–18
FOR KING AND COUNTRY

The coffin was carried from the Chapel and placed on a wagon drawn by six black artillery horses. Attending the ceremony was a representative of the King, Lieutenant General Sir George MacDonogh, and Marshal

Foch, who had led the French offensive against the Germans. They saluted the coffin before the procession moved off for the quayside. Following the coffin, French soldiers carried wreaths from the French Government and French and British service units, and behind them walked Marshal Foch and Lieutenant General MacDonogh. The procession was said to be a mile long and included disabled French soldiers, children, local dignitaries and ranks of French infantry and cavalry. Thousands stood and watched as the procession passed by. At the Quai Gambetta HMS *Verdun*, which was to bring the body home, waited. The ship had been specially chosen. It was named after the Battle of Verdun in 1916 at which Marshal Pétain had given the battle cry, 'On ne passe pas', ('They shall not pass'), to the French Army – a motto inscribed on the ship's quarter deck.

At the quayside Marshal Foch made a speech in which he expressed, 'the profound feelings of France for the invincible heroism of the British Army'. The body was, he said, a reminder 'to work in common to cement the victories we have gained by eternal union'. Lieutenant General MacDonogh thanked the Marshal on behalf of the King and the British Government. The bearer party, which had marched beside the wagon, carried the coffin on board as the ship's flag flew at half-mast. The wreaths and the sandbags of French soil followed. To the strains of 'God Save the King', and a 19-gun salute, HMS *Verdun* pulled slowly away.

The Unknown Warrior leaves the Chapel in Boulogne.

Earl Haig (front), and other military leaders, accompany the body to the Abbey.

Half-way across the Channel six British destroyers rendezvoused with HMS *Verdun*. With three line-abreast in front, and three behind, the convoy arrived in Dover.

A 19-gun salute greeted the ship, as did thousands who lined the quayside. At Dover the reception was purposely low-key; the main event was to be in London. Even so, it was a dignified and moving arrival. A military band played 'Land of Hope and Glory'. The coffin was carried to the station and put aboard a specially adapted luggage van – the same one which had carried the body of Nurse Edith Cavell home – which had been attached to the regular boat train service to London. Inside, its walls were draped in purple and there was a frieze of bay, chrysanthemums and rosemary. Alongside the coffin were placed the wreaths which had accompanied it on the ship, some so large it took four or five men to carry them. Four sentries stood guard until the train moved off. The top of the carriage had been painted white so that those who waited on bridges or other vantage points could tell which carriage held the Warrior. A second carriage was added for the accompanying military guard. Though this ceremony was special, the station staff had witnessed more than their share of grief during the war. Between 1915 and 1918 more than 7,500 ambulance trains had departed from Dover station carrying nearly 1,250,000 wounded. As the train pulled away the band played 'General Salute' and the Colours were lowered.

The train arrived at Victoria Station just after 8.30pm, and as crowds thronged the station, the carriages containing the Warrior and his military escort were shunted into the platform near the Buckingham Palace Road entrance to await the following day's ceremony.

The Burial

THROUGHOUT THE NIGHT OF 10/11 NOVEMBER, the body of the Unknown Warrior remained in the railway carriage at Victoria Station, guarded by soldiers from the Kings Company Grenadier Guards. At 9.15am the gun carriage and bearers were in position on the platform, with the massed bands of the guards division at the station entrance. In the carriage the coffin was prepared for the procession to the Abbey. The wreaths were removed and the coffin covered with a Union Flag, on which were placed a steel helmet and side arms. The flag had belonged to David Railton, the army chaplain who had originally written to the Dean suggesting the Abbey as a burial place for the Warrior. He was keen for his flag to be used, he said, as it had 'seen action'. He had often used it on the field of battle as a covering for the makeshift altars on which he would celebrate Holy Communion. The coffin was borne out of the van and placed on a gun carriage. From far away in Hyde Park came the sound of yet another 19-gun salute. As the gun carriage with its six black horses waited, 12 of the nation's highest ranking officers took their places either side of it, including Field Marshal Earl Haig and Admiral of the Fleet Earl Beatty. Behind the gun carriage came the mourners, including 400 ex-servicemen of mixed rank, marching four abreast. At 9.40am the procession moved off in slow time to the muffled sound of drums and of Chopin's Funeral March. Thousands of mourners stood in silence as the coffin passed them on its way up the Mall, through Admiralty Arch and down Whitehall.

At the newly erected Cenotaph, now covered with two large Union Flags, the carriage paused while King George V, dressed in the uniform of a Field Marshal, placed a wreath of red roses and bay leaves on the coffin. The inscription on the card, in his own hand, read:

A wreath from Queen Elizabeth II and The Duke of Edinburgh lies on the Grave.

OPPOSITE: President Obama lays a wreath at the Grave, as do all Heads of State on official visits to Britain.

> 'In proud memory of those warriors who died unknown in the Great War. Unknown and yet well known as dying and behold they lived. GEORGE R I'

In Whitehall, King George V lays his wreath on the Warrior's coffin.

After a hymn and a prayer, Big Ben chimed 11.00. On the last note the King pressed a button to release the two flags, and the Cenotaph was unveiled. After the King had laid a wreath against the Cenotaph, the procession moved off again to Westminster Abbey followed by the King, the Prince of Wales and his brothers, the Prime Minister, the Speaker of the House of Commons, and members of the Government. Waiting in the nave of the Abbey were Queen Mary, the Queen of Spain, and the Queen of Norway, who had travelled there by car from the Cenotaph in advance of the main procession. The congregation of the Abbey was made up of nearly a thousand widows and mothers of those killed in the War. As the Choir sang the burial sentences by Croft and Purcell, 'I am the resurrection and the life, saith the Lord', the coffin was carried from the north door through the quire and up the length of the nave which was lined by more than 100 holders of the Victoria Cross – the nation's highest bravery award.

When the coffin reached the graveside, a military band played Beethoven's *Equale for Trombones*. This was followed by the 23rd Psalm, 'The Lord is My Shepherd', and a lesson from the Book of Revelation read by the Dean. Then, as the Choir gently sang the hymn 'Lead, Kindly Light', the coffin was lowered into the grave. When the hymn had ended the King was handed a silver shell containing earth from a Flanders battlefield which he sprinkled on the coffin as the Dean said 'Earth to earth, ashes to ashes.' The service continued with the hymn 'Abide with me', there were more prayers and finally the hymn 'God of our fathers, known of old', by Rudyard Kipling. The Blessing and Reveille ended the service.

The Grave is prepared using soil brought from France.

BELOW: The chaplain's union flag which covered the coffin now hangs nearby.

After the service the Grave was covered with the Actors' Pall. This had been designed by Sir Ninian Comper and given to the Abbey by the Actors' Union in memory of their colleagues who had fallen in the War. Over this was placed the flag which had covered the coffin. The wreaths which had come over from France on HMS Verdun were laid round the Grave, four soldiers stood guard with arms reversed and the public was at last allowed in to file past the Grave. The queue stretched back as far as the Cenotaph.

Two men who, as boys, had been choristers at the service and who had witnessed the burial, wrote, 70 years later, about the impact the scene had had on them. Bill Wolferstan remembered wondering if the body could be that of his elder brother, Stanley. And the Rev'd Reginald Wright wrote, 'A feature that lives vividly in my mind was that after the service was over, thousands upon thousands of people streamed into the Abbey hour after hour, day after day, and when they got to the grave they cast their red poppies onto it. Gradually the area became a mass of red poppies. That spot, and everything associated with its presence in the Abbey, has become one that British people will always venerate and hold dear in their hearts and minds.' Another young chorister at the time recalled, many years later, entering the Abbey on the evening of the funeral after it had been closed to the public. 'It was in complete darkness save for the four candles round the grave where the soldiers were still standing, arms reversed. It made an indelible impression on me.'

At the end of the first week, on 18 November, the Grave was filled with the earth brought from France, and covered with a slab of Tournai marble

on which was written: 'A British Warrior who fell in The Great War 1914–18. For King and Country. Greater Love Hath No Man Than This.' A year later this was replaced by the black Belgium marble gravestone with the inscription we see today.

Close by the Grave are several objects associated with the Unknown Warrior. In the neighbouring Chapel, sometimes called the Warrior's Chapel, hangs David Railton's flag which had covered the coffin on its last journey to the Abbey. On Armistice Day 1921, exactly a year after the burial, it had been carried to the altar and dedicated by the Dean. On a nearby pillar hangs the ship's bell from HMS *Verdun*. The ship was broken up in 1946 but its bell was kept and given to the Abbey in 1990. Hanging against the opposite pillar is the American Congressional Medal of Honour, awarded to the Unknown Warrior by General Pershing in October 1921.

Despite the passing of the years, the Unknown Warrior's Tomb is as powerful a symbol now as it ever was. Uniquely, it is the only floor tomb in the Abbey which is never walked on. Even when the Abbey is transformed for a Coronation, a barrier protects it and the procession has to go round it.

The border of the stone reads:
X THE LORD KNOWETH THEM THAT ARE HIS X GREATER LOVE HATH NO MAN THAN THIS X UNKNOWN AND YET WELL KNOWN DYING AND BEHOLD WE LIVE X

BENEATH THIS STONE RESTS THE BODY
OF A BRITISH WARRIOR
UNKNOWN BY NAME OR RANK
BROUGHT FROM FRANCE TO LIE AMONG
THE MOST ILLUSTRIOUS OF THE LAND
AND BURIED HERE ON ARMISTICE DAY
11 NOV: 1920, IN THE PRESENCE OF
HIS MAJESTY KING GEORGE V
HIS MINISTERS OF STATE
THE CHIEFS OF HIS FORCES
AND A VAST CONCOURSE OF THE NATION

THUS ARE COMMEMORATED THE MANY
MULTITUDES WHO DURING THE GREAT
WAR OF 1914-1918 GAVE THE MOST THAT
MAN CAN GIVE LIFE ITSELF
FOR GOD
FOR KING AND COUNTRY
FOR LOVED ONES HOME AND EMPIRE
FOR THE SACRED CAUSE OF JUSTICE AND
THE FREEDOM OF THE WORLD

THEY BURIED HIM AMONG THE KINGS BECAUSE HE
HAD DONE GOOD TOWARD GOD AND TOWARD
HIS HOUSE

The bell from HMS *Verdun* and the American Congressional medal hang close by.

OPPOSITE: Wilfred Owen, commemorated with other war poets in Poets' Corner, was killed in the final week of the First World War.

Many countries now have their own Unknown Warrior to act as a focus for remembering their war dead. France buried its Unknown Warrior beneath the Arc de Triomphe at the same time as the British Warrior was buried. He was selected the day before in a similar way – one of eight bodies recovered from various battlefields, and chosen at random by a French soldier as the eight identical coffins lay side by side. The remaining seven bodies were buried together at the military cemetery at Verdun. In 1923 the French Minister of War, lit the eternal flame at the Arc de Triomphe.

Over the next two years, America, Belgium and Italy buried their own Unknown Soldiers. In 1921 the American Unknown Soldier was selected from one of four taken from graves in France. He was buried in the Arlington Military Cemetery. Italy's Unknown Soldier was buried in Rome in 1921, and Belgium's on 11 November 1922.

Many years later, Australia, Canada and New Zealand followed suit. Australia's Unknown Soldier was buried on 25 April 1993. He had been disinterred from the Adelaide Cemetery, Villers-Bretonneux, France – France being the theatre of war where more Australians have died in battle than any other. The Unknown Soldier was re-buried in the Australian War Memorial's Hall of Memory in Canberra.

Canada's Unknown Soldier was chosen in May 1999 from a grave in the region of Vimy Ridge, France – an area where many Canadians died – and flown to Ottawa for burial in the Hall of Honour in the Parliament Buildings. In 2001 a wreath of grasses and flora from Vimy Ridge was taken to Canada by Prince Charles to be laid on the Tomb. The wreath had rested on the Abbey's Unknown Warrior's Tomb from 9–14 April that year, the exact dates in 1917 of the battle of Vimy Ridge.

In 2003 New Zealand brought home an Unknown Soldier to be buried at the National War Memorial after a service at St Paul's Cathedral, Wellington.

ANTHEM FOR DOOMED YOUTH

Wilfred Owen

What passing bells for those who die as cattle?
    Only the monstrous anger of the guns,
    Only the stuttering rifles' rapid rattle
Can patter out their hasty orisons.
No mockeries for them from prayers or bells,
Nor any voice of mourning save the choirs, –
The shrill, demented choirs of wailing shells;
And bugles calling for them from sad shires.

What candles may be held to speed them all?
    Not in the hands of boys, but in their eyes
Shall shine the holy glimmer of good-byes.
    The pallor of girls' brows shall be their pall;
Their flowers the tenderness of patient minds,
And each slow dusk a drawing-down of blinds.

The Field of Remembrance

THE ARMISTICE WHICH ENDED THE FIRST WORLD WAR was signed in 1918 at the eleventh hour on the eleventh day of the eleventh month. Each year, on the anniversary of that moment, the nation pauses for a two-minute silence to remember the dead. In addition to the Cenotaph, the Unknown Warrior's Tomb and the thousands of War Memorials around the United Kingdom, there is another place where the nation mourns at this time of year: the Field of Remembrance in the shadow of Westminster Abbey. On the grass to the north of the Abbey – technically St Margaret's Churchyard – are laid out plots, each the size of a grave, in which members of the public and others with a particular reason to remember can plant a small cross. The Field is organised by the Royal British Legion, an organisation dedicated to helping old soldiers. At the Legion's Poppy Factory in Richmond, Surrey, disabled soldiers and their dependents produce the crosses and the millions of poppies which are sold each year to raise money to help disabled soldiers and those who depend on them.

The Field of Remembrance was started in 1928 by Major George Howson MC, the founder of the Legion's Poppy Factory. Together with a few disabled ex-servicemen from the Factory they gathered round a battlefield cross, familiar to those who had served in Flanders and on the Western Front, planted in St Margaret's Churchyard. There they sold poppies to passers-by and invited them to plant the poppy by the cross. The idea developed and eventually the Field of Remembrance assumed a more formal layout with no fewer than 250 plots. Each plot is sponsored by a particular regiment or group representing a particular interest. Alongside plots for famous regiments like The Coldstream Guards and the Life Guards, for example, are plots for the Army Film and Photographic Unit, London Transport, The Royal College of Midwives and the Russian Convoy Club. There is also a plot for crosses in memory of 'Civilians Killed by Enemy Action'. This plot has a particular relevance for Westminster Abbey because just inside the west doors of the Abbey is the official Roll of Honour of the Civilian War Dead killed in the Second World War. And just outside the west door, set into the ground, is a

Veterans and serving soldiers plant their crosses in the Field of Remembrance.

Sergeant
Gordon
Chandler

DAD - I
never knew
you but

I will
always
remember
you.

memorial in honour of the Innocent Victims of Oppression, Violence and War which was unveiled by Her Majesty the Queen on 10 October 1996.

Each year, a few days before Remembrance Sunday, a member of the Royal Family officially opens the Field of Remembrance by planting a cross in memory of the fallen. It was a duty performed for more than 50 years by Queen Elizabeth, the Queen Mother, until shortly before her death in 2002. The man who began it all, Major Howson, little realised how his idea would grow. In a letter to his parents written shortly after he had given a cheque for £2000 to start the poppy factory he wrote, 'I do not think it can be a great success, but it is worth trying. I consider the attempt ought to be made, if only to give the disabled their chance'.

Many of the crosses have poignant inscriptions.

OPPOSITE: Each year a member of the Royal Family officially opens the Field of Remembrance.

Acknowledgements

I am grateful to the following for their help: The Dean and Chapter of Westminster, Christine Reynolds, Sal Shuel, Simon Shuel, Gill Gibbins, Douglas East, Malcolm Crowthers, Paul Mellor and Craig McCarthy. I am particularly grateful to Andrew Dunsmore of Picture Partnership for his generosity over the use of his photographs of events which have taken place at the Abbey and at the Field of Remembrance. I also acknowledge with gratitude the following sources of information:

The Story of the Unknown Warrior by Michael Gavaghan, M & L Publications 1995;

The Unknown Warrior, published by the British Legion in the 1960s;

'The Unknown Warrior', an article published in *After the Battle* No. 6 1974 pages 48–53.

Picture acknowledgements:

© Getty Images: 10, 11, 12, 14, 15(top).

© Picture Partnership: 2, 13, 22, 23, back cover.

© Imperial War Museum: 6 (Q3014), 9 (Q31514).

© Dean and Chapter of Westminster (photo by Dave Lambert): 17.

Others by Malcolm Crowthers.

First published 2006
New edition 2013

ISBN 0–9552470–1–2
987–0–9552470–1–9

Design: Bridget Heal
Publisher: Tudsbury Press, 52 Thurleigh Road, London SW12 8UD
Printer: G H Smith & Son, Market Place, Easingwold, York YO61 3AB

OPPOSITE: The wreath from the Queen Mother's coffin was laid on the Tomb after her funeral service in 2002.